Immediate
Conversations 1

An English conversation textbook for beginners and false beginners

Scott Brown

John Brewer

Nigel Randell

Meiko Ikezawa

Jean-Luc Azra

Bruno Vannieu

For a presentation of the Immediate Method and information on teacher's set and distributor, see the last page of this book.

Contents

目次

イミディアット・カンバセーションズ 1

「イミディアット・カンバセーションズ」とは

英語の質問に答える時、不慣れな場合（特に初級）では、頭の中でまず日本語で答えを見つけ、それを英文に直すということをやっているので、答えるまでにずいぶん時間がかかってしまいます。しかし、「イミディアット・カンバセーションズ」ではこの時間をとらず、（＝ Immediate / イミディアット）しかも生きた会話ができるようになること、これを目指して私たちはこの教科書を「イミディアット・カンバセーションズ」と名づけました。

　この教科書を使った授業では、まず、**あなた自身のこと**について話します。そして、**先生やクラスメートといっしょに、身近な話題について**話します。このような経験を積み重ねて、英語で会話をするのに必要なことを学んでいきます。

・質問する

「どこに住んでいますか？」
「神戸です。」

・質問に答える

「納豆が好きですか？」
「はい、大好きです。」

・相手の言ったことに対して、反応する

「私はピアノとトランペットが演奏できます。」
「すごいですね！」

・質問されなくても、自分自身について話す

「僕の得意な教科は算数です」

　この教科書には、あなたが実際の会話を行う上で必要になることがふんだんに盛り込まれています。

　まず、あなたは「リアルタイム」で話すこと、つまり日本語に置き換えて考える時間を持たずに話すことを学びます。それから、自然な会話の流れの中で、新しい知識をどのように使っていくかを、少しずつ学んでいきます。こうして、会話を広げていくやり方を段階的に身につけていきます。といっても、難しく考える必要はありません。自分の毎日の生活のことを話したり、クラスメートに質問したりすることを通して、生きた会話を身につけていくのです。

沈黙と文化

■ 文化について

私たちは、幼い頃から「適切な話し方」に関するルールを教えられてきています。これは、社会の中での礼儀正しさのルールとして教えられるものです。このルールは、私たちの中に深く染み付いていて（つまりあまりに当たり前すぎて）、意識されることもあまりありません。そのため私たちは、会話のルールはどこでも同じで、自分の身につけた礼儀正しさに関するルールも世界中で通用すると考えがちです。

　しかし、これは真実ではありません。礼儀正しさのルールやその表現方法といったものは、文化や国によって大きく異なるものなのです。.

■ 日本では・・・

教室の中で先生が質問する時、当てられた生徒は答えを探すよう求められています。そのとき、よく生徒は長い時間考え込んだり、教科書を見たり、隣の生徒に答えを聞いたりしています。そのようにして答えを探している間、基本的に生徒は先生に対してずっと黙ったままです。または、そのまま長い間何も言わずに黙っていると、そのこと自体がひとつの答えとなります。つまり、「わかりません」という答えです。

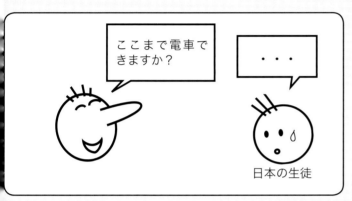
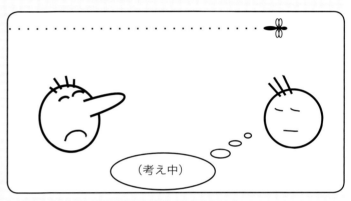

■ 他の国では・・・

　欧米を含む多くの他の国では、先生（またはクラスメート）が質問した場合、すぐに返答することが重要だとされています。質問されて黙っているのは、失礼な態度と見なされます。沈黙は、「あなたの質問には答えたくない」という意思の表れと解釈されるからです。一般社会でもそうなのですが、特に教室の中ではこのルールが重視されています。先生が質問したら、ほかの生徒を含めた全員があなたの答えを待っています。ここに文化の違いがあります。

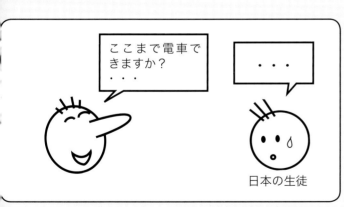
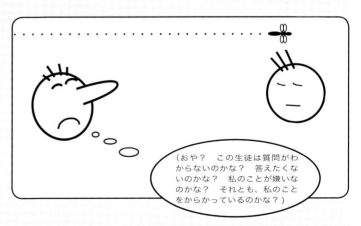

■ このクラスでは・・・

　できるだけ早く答えを言うように努力しましょう。できれば、5秒以内に。最初は難しいと感じるかもしれませんが、慣れれば大丈夫！　それに他の国ではみんなそうしているのだから、このスピードについていけるようにがんばりましょう。でも、もしも答えがわからなかったら？　あるいは、質問が早すぎて理解できなかったら？　そんなときのための、簡単で効果的な方法はいくつもあります。私たちは、もちろんそのようなことも練習します。

■ **先生が言ったことでわからないことがあったら**、そのわからなかった言葉の意味を先生に質問しましょう。先生は、ほかの言い方やジェスチャーで、あるいはイラストで説明してくれます。場合によっては、日本語で教えてくれることもあるでしょう。また、「辞書で調べなさい」とか、「クラスメートにきいてみなさい」と指示を出してくれます。会話の流れを中断させないこと。言葉がずっと続いていること。それが大切です。

「何か楽器ができますか？」

「「musical instruments（ミュージカル・インスツルメンツ）って、日本語で言うと何ですか？」

■ **先生が言ったことで聞き取れない言葉があったら**、先生に質問を繰り返してくれるように頼みましょう。これは、たった１つの言葉、「Sorry?（えっ？）」でできてしまいます。

「ブラッド・ピットって、知っていますか？」

「えっ？」

「ブラッド・ピットって、知っていますか？」

■ **質問の内容はわかったけど、答えを英語でどう言うか知らないので答えられない。**そんなときには、それを英語でどう言えばいいのか、先生に聞きましょう。

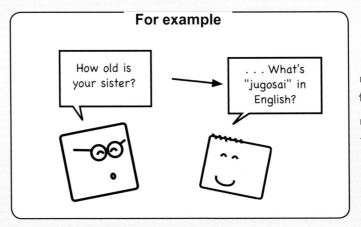

「お姉さんは何才ですか？」

「「15才」って、英語でどう言うんですか？」

■ **質問の内容はわかったけど、答えが思いつかない。** そんな場合には、「I don't know（わかりません）」と言いましょう。あなたの言い方と態度に相手を尊重するものがあれば、英語ではこれも立派な答えとなります。黙ったままでいるよりも、これははるかに礼儀正しい態度なのです。

「「私は東京に住んでいます」は英語でどう言いますか？」

「わかりません。」

　質問の答えがわかっているときは、もちろんすぐにそれを言いましょう。自分の答えが正しいかどうか自信がない場合でも、とにかく口に出して言ってみましょう。もし間違いがあったとしても先生が直してくれます。これを繰り返すことが、うまく話せるようになるための近道です。

会話トレーニング

　学習した内容を実際の会話の中で使っていき、即座に言えるようになるためには、たくさんの経験（会話トレーニング）を重ねる必要があります。知っている単語の数を増やしたり、新しい表現の構造を理解したりする上で、英語を書く練習が重要であることは言うまでもありません。しかし、リアルタイムで話せるようになるためには、やはり会話を繰り返し実践することが必要です。また、英文の読解によって単語や文章を理解できるようになれたとしても、残念ながらそれだけでは話せるようにはなれないのです。

　この教科書を使った授業で、これからあなたはクラスメートといっしょにたくさんの会話トレーニングを行います。クラスメートに質問し、それに答えてもらう。逆に、クラスメートからの質問に、あなたが答えます。これをできるだけ何回も、そして学習した単語や表現をできるだけ駆使して、練習してください。たとえば「Does your father have a hobby?（お父さんは何か趣味を持っていますか？）」、「Does your mother have a hobby?（お母さんは何か趣味を持っていますか？）」、「Does your brother have a hobby?（お兄さんは何か趣味を持っていますか？）」、「Does your father speak any foreign languages?（お父さんは外国語を話せますか）」、「Does your mother drive?（お母さんは車を運転しますか？）」などのように。やがて、このようなやり取りがスムーズにできるようになったら、次はお互いにクイズ形式で会話してみましょう。「What's『お子さんは何才ですか』in English?（『お子さんは何才ですか』は英語でどう言いますか？）」、「What's『お兄さんは何才ですか』in English?（『お兄さんは何才ですか』は英語でどう言いますか？）」などのように。一人が質問し、相手が答えます。そして、次にその役割を交代します。

会話を楽しみましょう！

　この教科書は「イミーディアット・メソッド」と呼ばれる外国語教授法に基いて作られています。この教授法は日本で開発され、英語だけでなく、フランス語やドイツ語、日本語での会話能力を身につけるために、現在たくさんの学習者が実践しています。これらの学習者にとって、イミーディアット・メソッドはけっして難しいものではなく、逆に誰もが「とても楽しい！」と評価しています。

　これからあなたも、英語でのやり取りを通じて、クラスメートや先生について多くのことを発見していくことでしょう。そして、先生やクラスのみんなに、あなた自身のことを英語で言ってみてください。すぐにあなたは、外国語で話すことはそれほど難しいことではないと理解できるようになるはずです。英語での会話を、大いに楽しんでください！

Immediate Conversations 1

Immediate Conversations

This book is called "Immediate Conversations" because it teaches you to speak English immediately, in real-time conversations! This book is not like other books. You will talk about **yourselves**, and find out interesting information about the **daily lives** of your classmates .

You will practice the following elements of conversation:

- **Asking questions:**

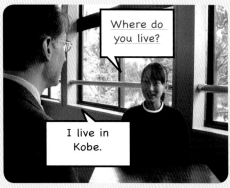

- **Answering questions:**

- **Reacting to what your partner said:**

- **Speaking about yourself without being asked a question:**

This book gives you all you need to conduct real conversations!

- First, you learn to speak in "real time," without pausing to think.
- Then, little by little, you learn how to use your new knowledge in natural conversations, just like a native speaker. It's easy when you are talking about real life, and asking meaningful questions to your classmates.

Silence and Culture

■ Polite expression and culture

In our own society we learn the appropriate way to use the rules of politeness in speech from an early age. These rules have become deeply internalized. They are automatic, and are used subconsciously. We generally have the impression that these rules are the same everywhere, that they are universal and do not change from place to place. But this is not true: rules of politeness are cultural. This means that people express politeness differently depending on the country and culture they belong to.

■ In Japan

In Japan when someone is asked a question in class, that person is expected to come up with an answer, but it is not unusual for that person to think for a long time, gaze into in their textbook or even consult a classmate next to them. The entire time they are searching for the answer, they remain silent. This silence may have a meaning in itself: It could mean "I am not able to answer the question."

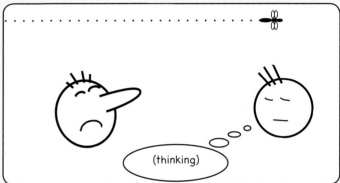

■ Outside Japan

In the West, when your teacher (or someone else) asks you a question, it is important that you answer almost immediately. Remaining silent when you have been asked a question is considered impolite. It is interpreted as "I don't want to answer you". This is true for normal conversation, and it is even more important in class, when your teacher asks a question and everyone is waiting for the response. It is a cultural difference.

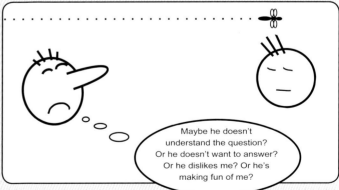

■ In this class

We will make an effort to answer questions very quickly, within five seconds. It might be difficult for you at first, but this is the way people do it in the West. How can you do this if you don't know the answer, or haven't understood the question? There are a number of simple ways, and we will practice them.

■ **If you don't understand something the teacher says,** just ask the meaning of the words you didn't understand. Your teacher can explain with a sentence, with gestures, with a drawing, or give you the Japanese equivalent. The teacher might also ask you to look a word up in the dictionary, or have you ask someone else in the class. Each time, the verbal exchange is successful, and the conversation can continue.

■ **If you don't hear something the teacher says,** just ask the teacher to repeat the question! You can do it with one word: "Sorry?"

■ **If you do understand the question, but you can't answer because you don't know how to say something in English,** just ask how to say the word (or sentence) in English!

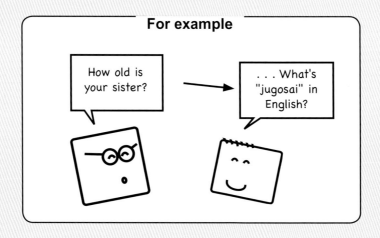

■ **If you understand the question but you don't know the answer,** just say "I don't know" If your voice and demeanor is respectful, this is a perfectly polite way to answer in English. It is infinitely more polite than remaining silent.

Of course, if you are asked a question and know the answer, say it right away! Even if you are not sure the answer is correct, say it anyway. The teacher will correct mistakes if there are any. This is the time when you will learn the most!

Conversation Practice

To use what you learn in real conversations, it is necessary to do a lot of conversation practice so you can say things immediately. Written exercises are important for remembering vocabulary and new sentence structures, but it is conversation practice that will allow you to speak in real time. If you only know a word or a sentence from reading, you will not be able to say it without hesitation. You have to do a lot of oral practice with your partner in class. The basic procedure for doing this is that you ask a given question to your partner, and your partner answers. Then you reverse roles: your partner will ask you a question, and you answer. Do this as much as you can, using all the possible variations you have learned. For example: "Does your father have a hobby?", "Does your mother have a hobby?", "Does your brother have a hobby?", "Does your father speak any foreign languages?", "Does your mother drive?", etc. When you have exhausted this type of conversation practice, you can quiz each other: "What's "anata no kodomotachi wa ikutsu desuka" in English?", "What' s 'anata no onii-san wa ikutsu desuka' in English?", etc. One partner asks the questions, the other answers. Then you exchange roles.

Have Fun!

The *Immediate Method* is the teaching method on which this book is based. It was developed in Japan, and many beginning students have used it to learn to speak French, German and English. They all say that it is not very difficult and that it is a lot of fun! You will also have the enjoyment of learning all kinds of things about your classmates and your teacher, and the pleasure of telling them about yourself! Most of all, you will realize that it is not so difficult to have conversations in a foreign language. Have fun!

How to use this book

Two CD tracks for each Grammar toolbox:
付属 CD には、ひとつの Grammar toolbox（文型図）につき、解説と例文の合計 2 トラックが収録されています。

- one with a simple explanation in Japanese of the main grammar point, and sometimes some practical advice
  重要な文法事項に関する日本語による解説、および会話をする際のアドバイス
- one with possible sentences that can be made with the combination of the Grammar toolbox and the Vocabulary boxes.
  Grammar toolbox（文型図）と Vocabulary boxes（単語集）の各要素を使ってできる例文

The printed numbers are the track numbers of the CD.
各ページに出てくる CD マークの数字が、CD のトラックナンバーを示しています。

Grammar toolbox:
(文型図)

gives you the main structure(s).
文の組み立て方を、わかりやすく図で示しています。
White arrows are for questions, black arrows for answers.
白い矢印に続く文が質問、黒い矢印に続く文がその答えです。

Vocabulary:
(単語集)

by varying the words, you can make many different sentences. Your teacher can give you new vocabulary, or ask you to think about possible words. Write the new words and their Japanese equivalent here.
単語を変えていくことで、たくさんの文章を作ることができます。先生が新しい単語を教えてくれますが、使うことのできる単語をできるだけ自分で考えてみるようにしましょう。新しい単語が出てきたら、日本語訳といっしょに、ここに書き込んでいってください。

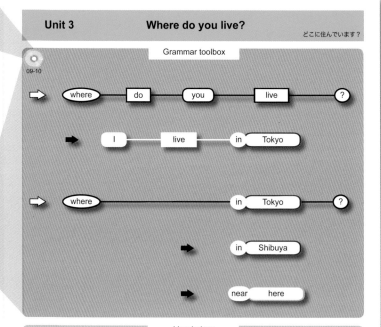

Unit 3 — **Where do you live?** — どこに住んでいます？

Grammar toolbox (09-10)

⇨ where — do — you — live — ?
➡ I — live — in — Tokyo

⇨ where — in — Tokyo — ?
➡ in — Shibuya
➡ near — here

Vocabulary

Tokyo prefecture	東京		here	ここ
Osaka prefecture			Yokohama park	
Hokkaido			Tokyo dome	
California			Koshien stadium	
Nara			Osaka station	
Nagoya			Heian shrine	

14

この教科書の使い方

Examples:
（会話例）

examples of the main exchanges that can be made with this lesson.
会話の流れの例をマンガで示しています。

Comparing languages:
（言語の比較）

In this space, you can write sentences in English and Japanese, and compare how to express things in the two languages. Pick up sentences from the CD, or sentences that your teacher dictates to you. You can also make new sentences by using the words and structures from the Grammar Toolboxes and Vocabulary Boxes.
ここに、英語と日本語で文を書いて、表現の仕方を比べてみましょう。例えば、CD の文を聞き取って、または先生が読むのを聞き取って書いてみましょう。Grammar toolbox（文型図）と Vocabulary boxes（単語集）から言葉を選んで文を作ってみることもできます。

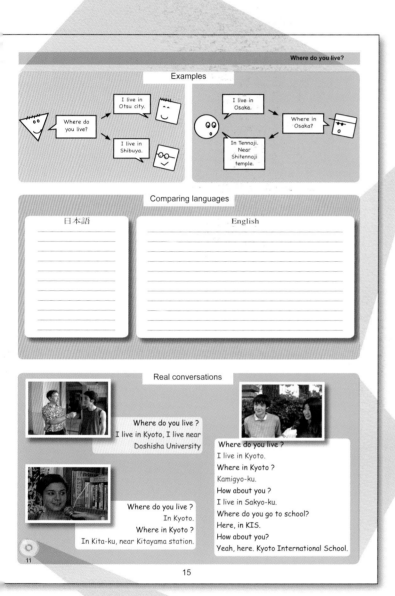

Real conversations:
（実際の会話例）

transcripts of real video interviews we made using questions from this lesson. Your teacher can show you the video in class. You will hear a variety of accents of English spoken by people from different countries.
レッスンで習う質問を使って、実際にインタビューをしてみました。授業ではそのビデオを一緒に見ていきます。国が変わると、話される英語のアクセントもずいぶん違うことがわかるでしょう。

One CD track
CD

Interviews have been re-recorded for the CD, by native speakers from three different countries: America, New Zealand and England.
Interviews are numbered in the order they appear on the CD.
このインタビューの内容を、CD で聴くことができます。答えているのは３カ国（アメリカ、ニュージーランド、イギリス）のネイティブ・スピーカーです。CD には、写真の番号順に録音されています。

Unit 1   What's " 車 " in English?

Grammar toolbox 1

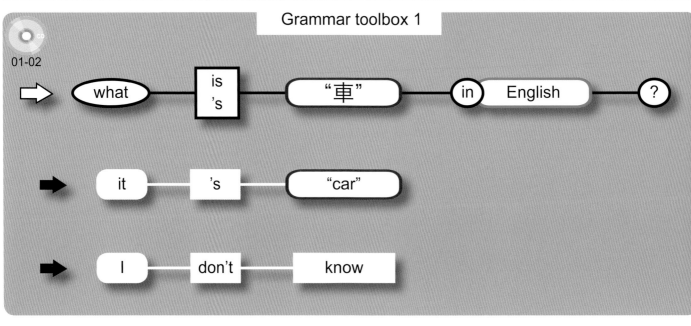

01-02

what — is/'s — "車" — in English — ?

it — 's — "car"

I — don't — know

Vocabulary

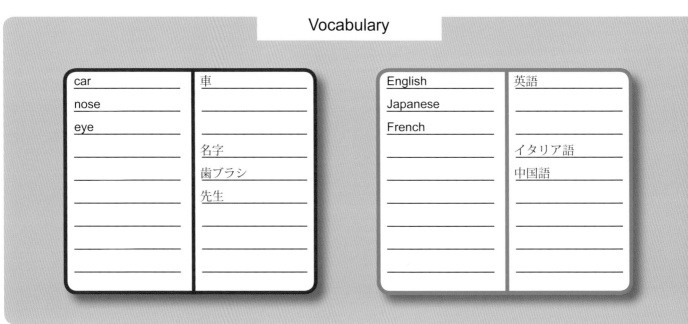

car	車
nose	
eye	
	名字
	歯ブラシ
	先生

English	英語
Japanese	
French	
	イタリア語
	中国語

Grammar toolbox 2

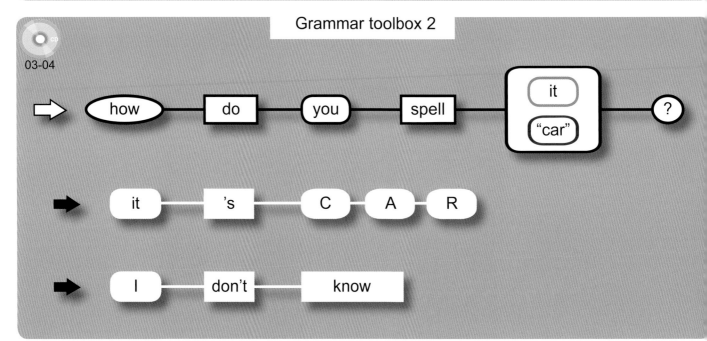

03-04

how — do — you — spell — it / "car" — ?

it — 's — C — A — R

I — don't — know

14

Examples

What's "sensei" in English?
- I don't know.
- It's "teacher".

What's 'konnichiwa' in French?
- I don't know.
- It's "bonjour".

What's "neko" in English?
How do you spell it?
- It's "cat".
- It's "C-A-T".

How do you spell "eye"?
How do you spell "eye"?
- Sorry?
- It's "E-Y-E".

Comparing languages

日本語	English

Real conversations

Do you speak Japanese ?
A little bit.
What's "cat" in Japanese ?
I don't know !

What's "kuruma" in English?
It's "car".
What's "kuruma" in French?
It's "voiture".

What's "densha" in English?
"Train".
How do you spell that?
T-R-A-I-N.

What's your name?

Grammar toolbox

06-07

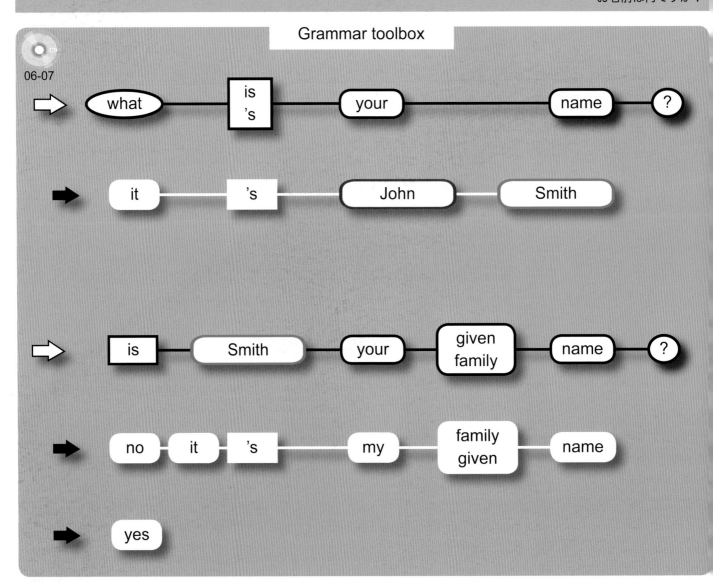

Vocabulary

John	ジョン		Smith	スミス
Peter			Johnson	
Junko			Tanaka	
	恵美子			木下
	サム			大川

Examples

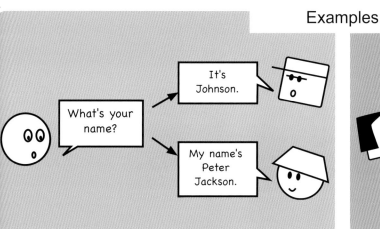

What's your name?

It's Johnson.

My name's Peter Jackson.

Is Fred your family name?

No, it's my given name.

Comparing languages

日本語

English

Real conversations

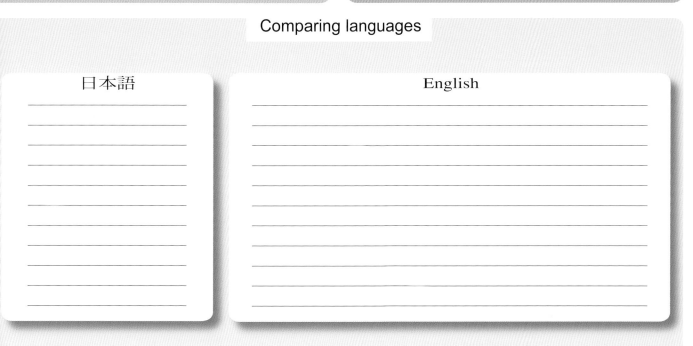

1

What's your name?
Philip.
What's your name?
Constance.
How do you spell that?
C-O-N-S-T-A-N-C-E.

3

What's your name?
My name's Jules.
How do you spell that?
J-U-L-E-S.

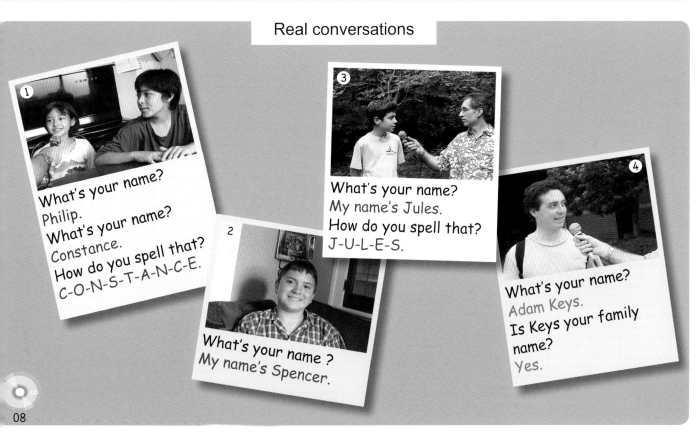

2

What's your name ?
My name's Spencer.

4

What's your name?
Adam Keys.
Is Keys your family name?
Yes.

Grammar toolbox

09-10

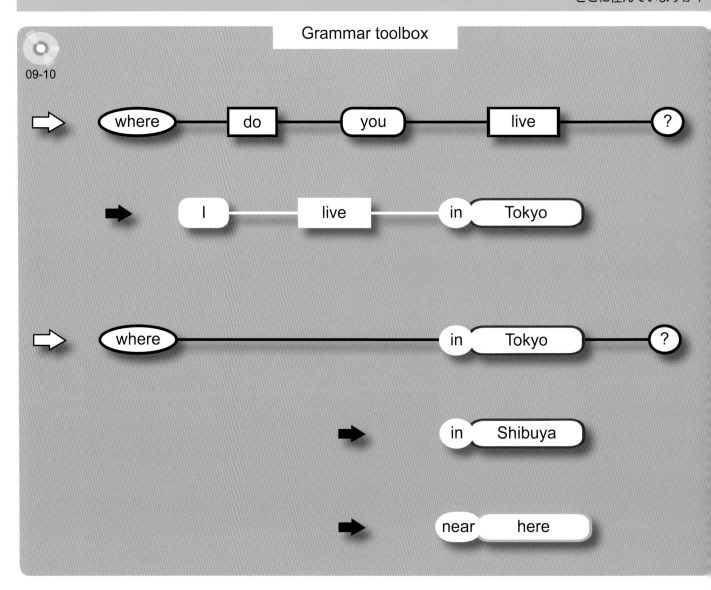

Vocabulary

Tokyo prefecture	東京都
Osaka prefecture	
Hokkaido	
California	
Nara	
Nagoya	

here	ここ
Yokohama park	
Tokyo dome	
Koshien stadium	
Osaka station	
Heian shrine	

Examples

I live in Otsu city.

Where do you live?

I live in Shibuya.

I live in Osaka.

Where in Osaka?

In Tennoji. Near Shitennoji temple.

Comparing languages

日本語

English

Real conversations

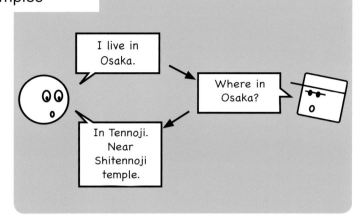

Where do you live?
I live in Kyoto, I live near Doshisha University.

Where do you live?
I live in Kyoto.
Where in Kyoto?
Kamigyo-ku.
How about you?
I live in Sakyo-ku.
Where do you go to school?
Here, in KIS.
How about you?
Yeah, here. Kyoto International School.

Where do you live?
In Kyoto.
Where in Kyoto?
In Kita-ku, near Kitayama station.

11

Grammar toolbox 1

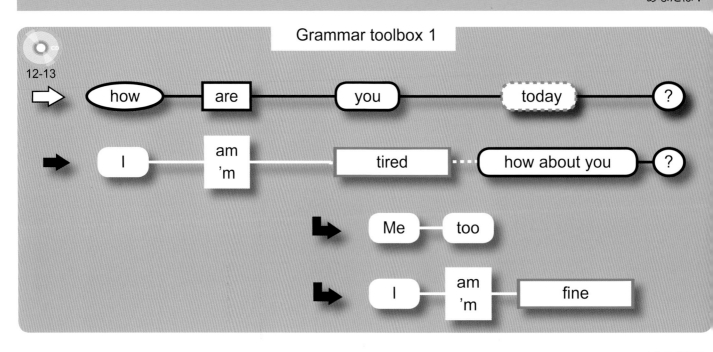

12-13

how — are — you — today — ?

I — am / 'm — tired ---- how about you — ?

Me — too

I — am / 'm — fine

Vocabulary

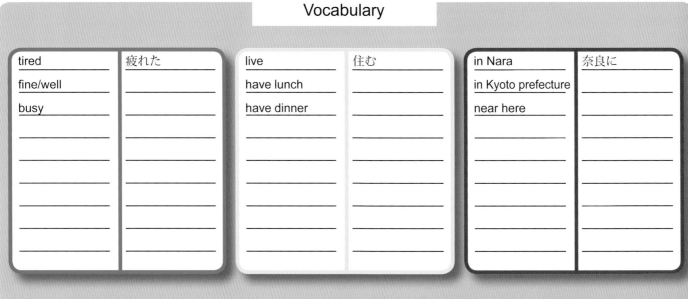

tired	疲れた	live	住む	in Nara	奈良に
fine/well		have lunch		in Kyoto prefecture	
busy		have dinner		near here	

Grammar toolbox 2

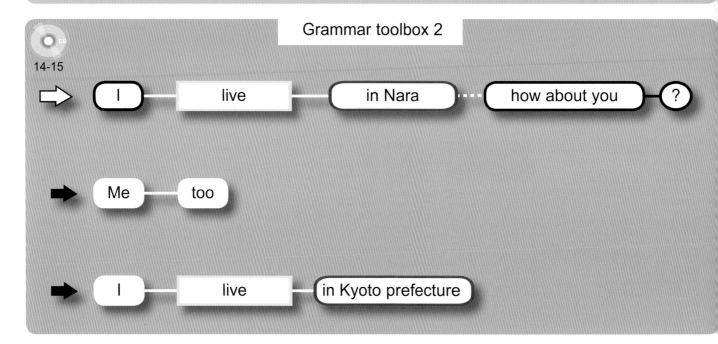

14-15

I — live — in Nara ---- how about you — ?

Me — too

I — live — in Kyoto prefecture

Examples

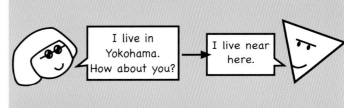

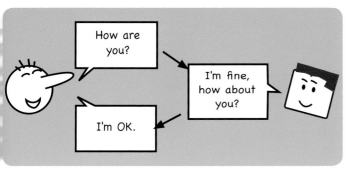

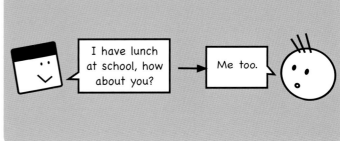

Comparing languages

日本語	English

Real conversations

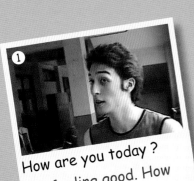

How are you today?
I'm feeling good. How about you?
I'm not bad.

I live in Kyoto. How about you?
Oh, me too! But I work in Kobe.

Where do you live?
In Shiga prefecture, in Otsu.
And how about you?
I live in Kyoto.

Grammar toolbox

17-18

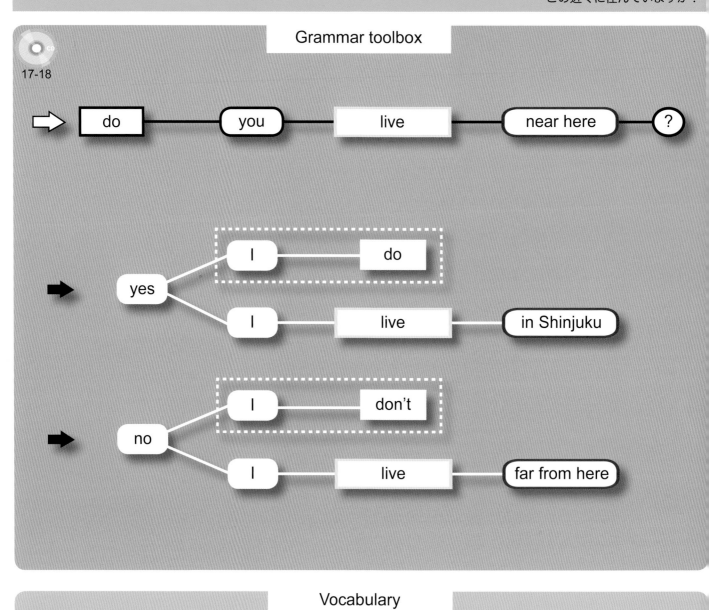

Vocabulary

live	住む		near here	この近く
work			in Shinjuku	
go to cram school			far from here	

Examples

Comparing languages

日本語

English

Real conversations

Do you live near here?
Yes, I do.
Where?
In Yamashina.
I see.

Do you live in Japan ?
Yes, I live in Kyoto.
Where, in Kyoto?
In Kita-ku.

Do you work near here?
No, I work far from here,
in Kobe. How about you?
Me too!

19

Grammar toolbox

20-21

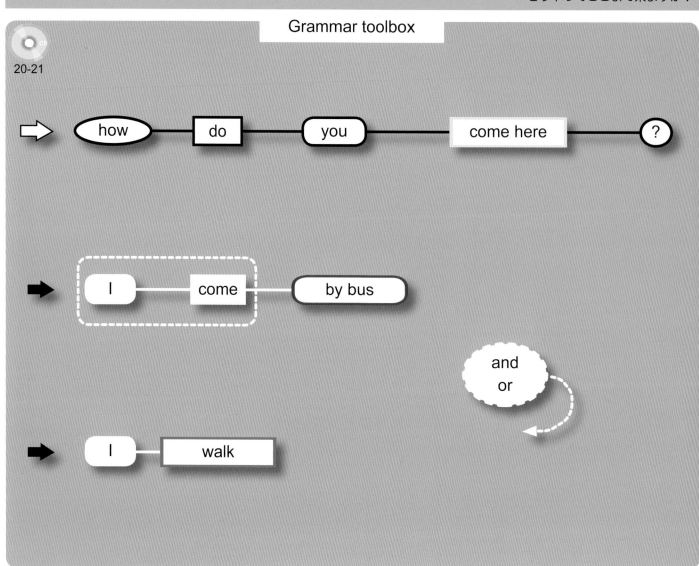

Vocabulary

come here	ここまで来る	by bus	バスで	walk	歩く
come to work		by train		cycle	
go to work		on foot		drive	

Examples

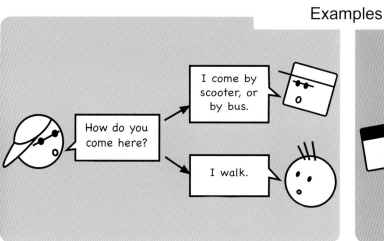

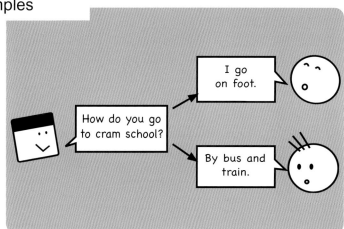

Comparing languages

日本語	English

Real conversations

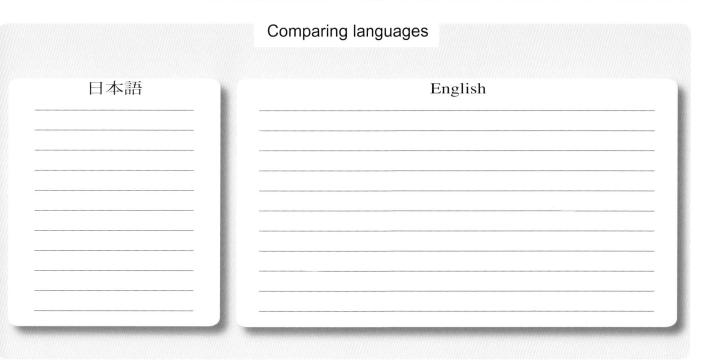

1. How do you come to work?
By subway and by bus.

2. How do you go to school, Matt?
I drive my car.

3. How do you go shopping?
I walk.

4. How do you come to school?
Sometimes I come by car, and sometimes I come by bus and train.

Grammar toolbox 1

23-24

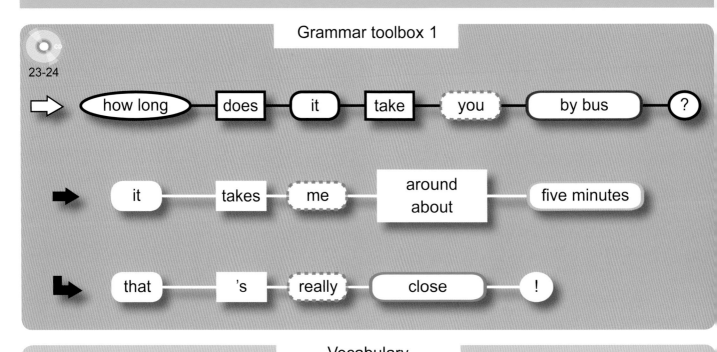

→ (how long) — [does] — (it) — [take] — ⟨ you ⟩ — (by bus) — (?)

➡ (it) — [takes] — ⟨ me ⟩ — [around / about] — (five minutes)

➡ (that) — ['s] — ⟨ really ⟩ — (close) — (!)

Vocabulary

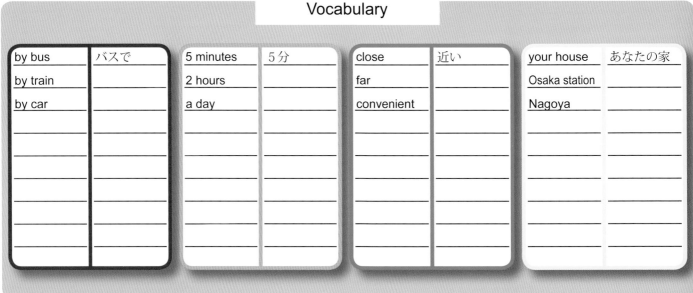

by bus	バスで	5 minutes	5分	close	近い	your house	あなたの家
by train		2 hours		far		Osaka station	
by car		a day		convenient		Nagoya	

Grammar toolbox 2

25-26

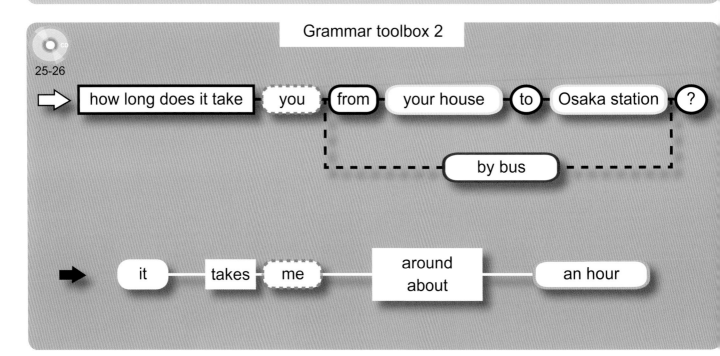

→ [how long does it take] — ⟨ you ⟩ — (from) — (your house) — (to) — (Osaka station) — (?)
(by bus)

➡ (it) — [takes] — ⟨ me ⟩ — [around / about] — (an hour)

Examples

Comparing languages

日本語	English

Real conversations

How do you go to school?
By bicycle.
How long does it take?
Thirty minutes.

Where are you from?
I'm from Australia.
How long does it take to get from
Australia to Japan?
It takes about ten hours by plane.

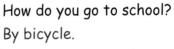

Where do you work ?
In Kobe.
How long does it take you
from your house to Kobe ?
It takes two hours.
Wow, that's really long!

Grammar toolbox 1

28-29

do — you — like — swimming — ?
like — movies — ?

yes — I — like — it
them

no — I — don't like — it
them

Vocabulary

swimming	水泳
English	
jogging	

movies	映画
cats	
dogs	

Grammar toolbox 2

30-31

do — you — like — swimming — ?
movies — ?

yes — I — like / love — it / them

no — I — hate — it / them
➤ Me — too

no — I — don't like — it / them
➤ Me — neither

Examples

Comparing languages

日本語	English

Real conversations

Unit 9   What's your favorite sport?

一番好きなスポーツは何ですか？

Grammar toolbox

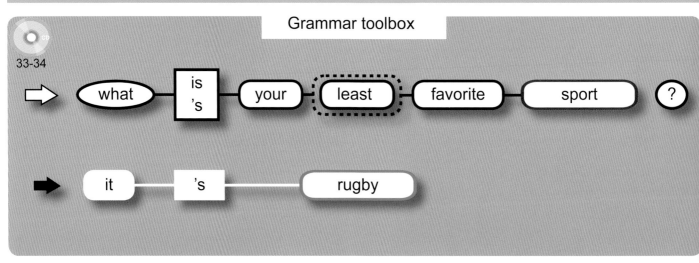

33-34

Vocabulary

sport	スポーツ
_____	_____
_____	_____

rugby	ラグビー
_____	_____
_____	_____

subject	科目
_____	_____
_____	_____

English	英語
_____	_____
_____	_____

animal	動物
_____	_____
_____	_____

cats	猫
_____	_____
_____	_____

_____	_____
_____	_____
_____	_____

_____	_____
_____	_____
_____	_____

_____	_____
_____	_____
_____	_____

_____	_____
_____	_____
_____	_____

Notes

Examples

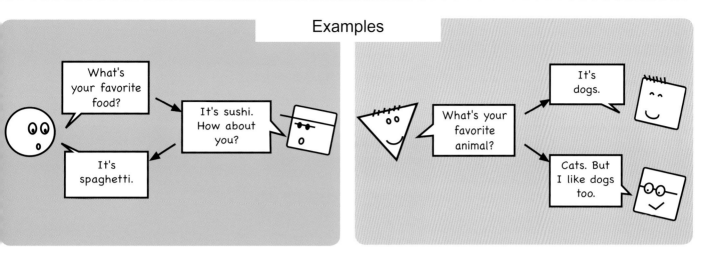

What's your favorite food?

It's sushi. How about you?

It's spaghetti.

What's your favorite animal?

It's dogs.

Cats. But I like dogs too.

Comparing languages

日本語	English

Real conversations

What's your least favourite subject?
Math.
How about you?
Math!

What's your favorite vegetable ?
It's potatoes.
What's your least favorite vegetable ?
I don't know.

Do you like math?
No, I don't like it.
What's your favourite subject?
It's art.

What's your favorite animal ?
Definitely the marmot.

35

31

Grammar toolbox 1

36-37

do — you — have — any brothers and sisters — ?

yes — I — have

an   older sister

a   younger brother

two / three   brothers   sisters

and

no — I — don't have — any brothers and sisters

Vocabulary

brothers and sisters	兄弟	younger brother	弟	computer	コンピューター
pets		older sister		dog	
children		goldfish		golden retriever	

Grammar toolbox 2

38-39

do — you — have — a computer — ?

yes — I — have

one

a   laptop

no but I — have — a mobile phone

32

Examples

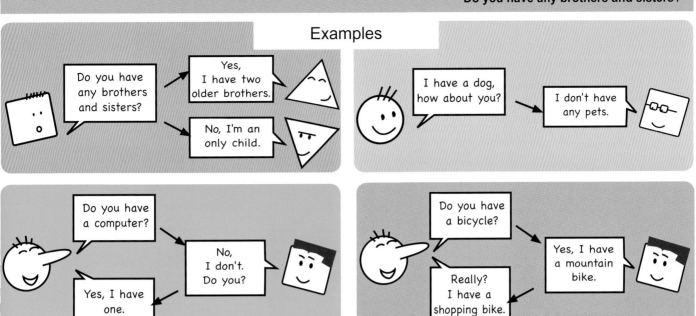

Comparing languages

日本語

English

Real conversations

① Do you have any brothers and sisters?

I have two sisters.

Yes, I have two brothers and one sister.

Yes, I have an older sister.

2

Do you have any pets?
I have four pets, I have two dogs and two cats.

3

Do you have a computer?
Yes, I have a laptop and a desktop.

40

What's your sister's name?

あなたのお姉さん／妹の名前は何ですか？

Grammar toolbox

41-42

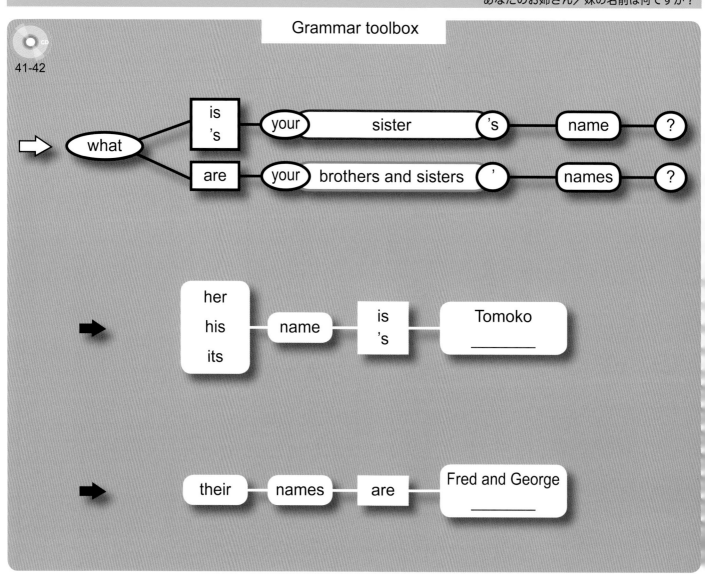

Vocabulary

sister	姉／妹
brother	
daughter	

brothers and sisters	兄弟
parents	
pets	

Examples

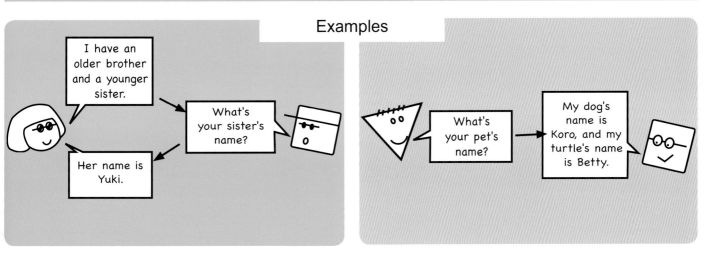

Comparing languages

日本語

English

Real conversations

What's your brother's name?
His name is Yukio.

Do you have any children?
Yes, I have a daughter and two sons.
What are your children's names?
Jessica, Noah and Sam.

Do you have any pets?
Yes, I have a dog. I have a
Labrador.
What's your dog's name?
Her name is Nana.

What are your parents' names ?
Charles and Mieko.

43

Grammar toolbox 1

44-45

do — you

play	baseball
	(the) piano
do	kendo
swim	

?

yes — I — do

no — I — don't

Vocabulary

baseball	野球		piano	ピアノ		kendo	剣道		swim	泳ぐ
soccer			guitar			judo			jog	
volleyball			recorder			track and field			ski	

Grammar toolbox 2

46-47

do — you — play — any — sports / instruments — ?

play	soccer
	(the) guitar
do	judo
jog	

yes — I — sometimes

no — I — don't

Examples

Comparing languages

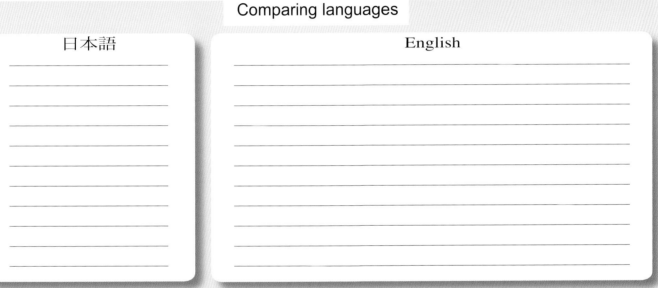

日本語

English

Real conversations

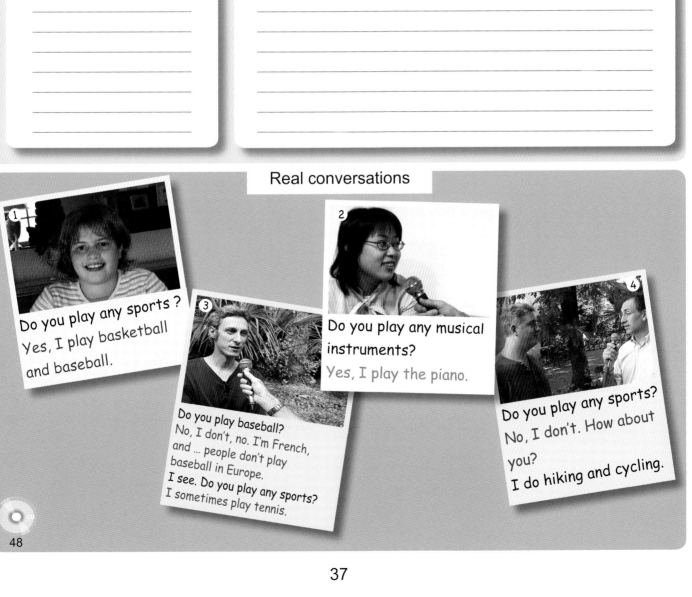

1. Do you play any sports? Yes, I play basketball and baseball.

3. Do you play baseball? No, I don't, no. I'm French, and ... people don't play baseball in Europe. I see. Do you play any sports? I sometimes play tennis.

2. Do you play any musical instruments? Yes, I play the piano.

4. Do you play any sports? No, I don't. How about you? I do hiking and cycling.

48

37

Grammar toolbox

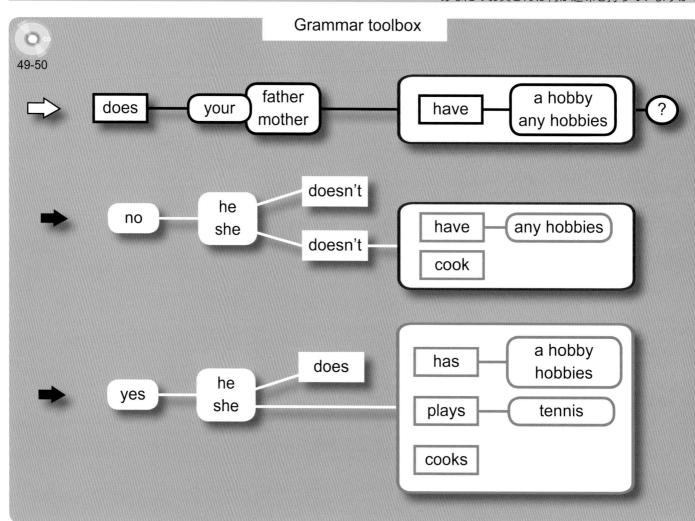

Vocabulary

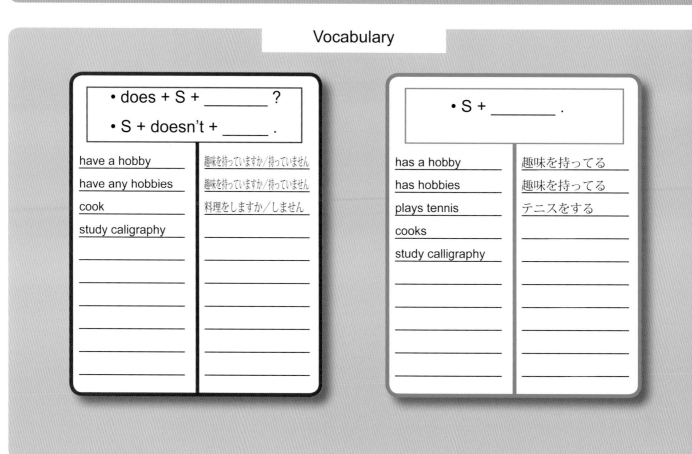

• does + S + _____ ?	
• S + doesn't + _____ .	

have a hobby	趣味を持っていますか/持っていません
have any hobbies	趣味を持っていますか/持っていません
cook	料理をしますか/しません
study caligraphy	

• S + _____ .	

has a hobby	趣味を持ってる
has hobbies	趣味を持ってる
plays tennis	テニスをする
cooks	
study calligraphy	

Examples

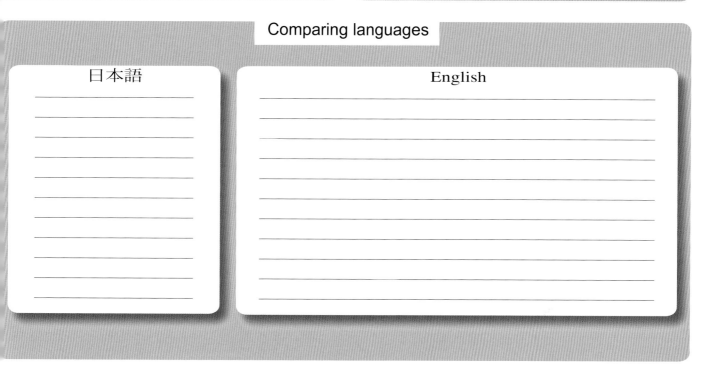

Does your mother have a hobby?

Yes, she studies caligraphy.

I don't know.

My father doesn't speak any foreign languages. Does your father speak English?

Yes, he speaks English a little bit.

Comparing languages

日本語

English

Real conversations

Does your father have a hobby?
Um, he plays the bass.
I see, is he pretty good?
Ah yeah, he's pretty good.

Does your father have a hobby?
Ah, not that I know of.
How about your mother?
She likes reading books.
How about you, does your father have a hobby?
He might, but I don't know.
How about your mother?
I have no idea.

Do you have a hobby?
Yeah, I like to build model planes and cars.
Great, does your Dad have a hobby?
No.
Does your mother have a hobby?
Not that I know of.
I see.

51

Grammar toolbox 1

52-53

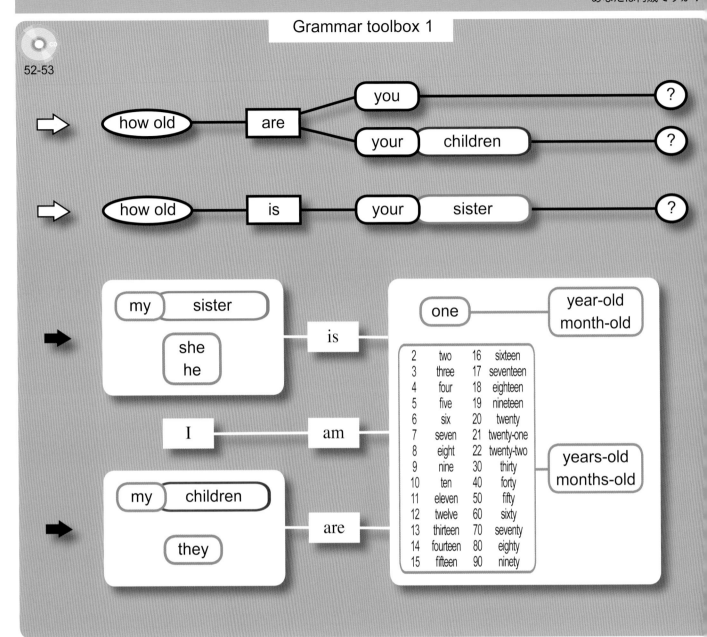

Vocabulary

children	子供		sister	姉／妹
brothers and sisters			brother	
parents			son	

Examples

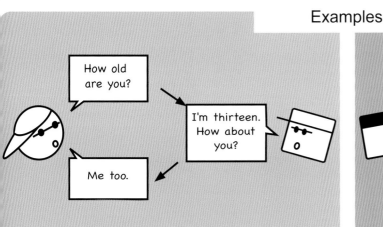

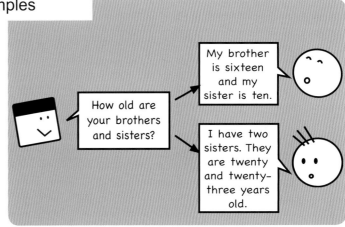

Comparing languages

日本語	English

Real conversations

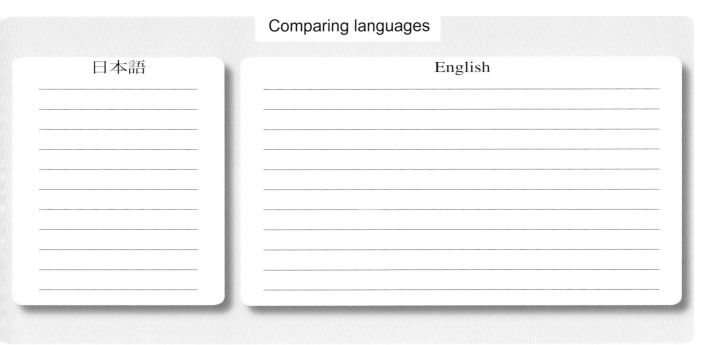

1 How old are you, Spencer?
I'm 13 years-old.
How old are your sisters?
Mckenzie is 10, and Sherryl is 7.

3 How old are you?
Nine.
And how about you?
Eleven years-old.

2 How old are your children?
They are 9 years-old and 5 years-old.

4 What's your best friend's name?
Sarah.
How old is Sarah?
Twenty-two.
How old are you?
Oh, it's a secret!

Grammar toolbox

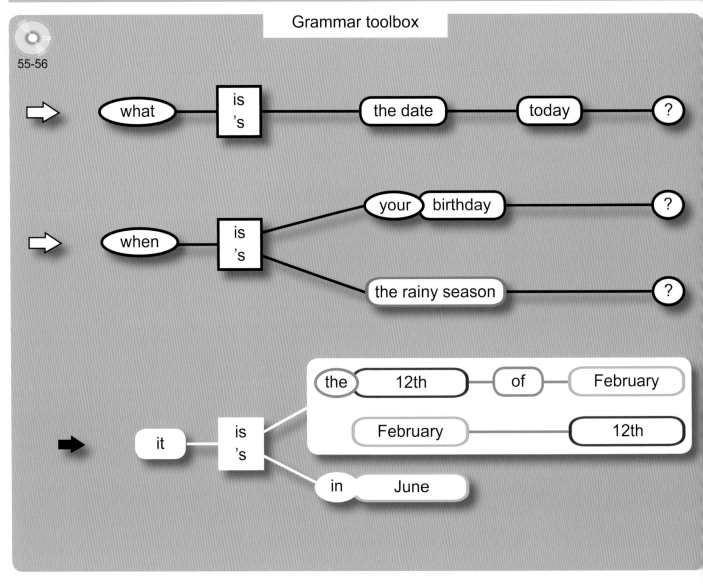

Vocabulary

the rainy season	梅雨	1st first	1日	January	1月
Mother's day		2nd second		February	
Valentine's day		3rd third		March	

Examples

Comparing languages

日本語	English

Real conversations

1
When is your birthday ?
January 17th.
When is your sister's birthday ?
Uhmm, June 30th... I think!

How old are you?
I can't answer that!
When is your birthday?
It's in August.

3
How old are you?
I'm 14.
When is your birthday?
It's July 28th.

4
When is the school festival at Kyoto University?
It's in November.

57

43

Grammar toolbox 1

58-59

→ do you know | who | Brad Pitt | is | ?

→ yes | she / he | is / 's | an actor / a Japanese actor / the Japanese Prime Minister

→ no | who | is | he / she | ?

Vocabulary

Brad Pitt	ブラッドピット		actor	俳優		Japanese Prime Minister	総理大臣		Paris	パリ
Julia Roberts			actress			American President			Belgium	
			American singer			math teacher			France	
									Brussels	

Grammar toolbox 2

60-61

→ do you know | where | Paris | is | ?
do you know | what | the capital | of | Belgium | is | ?

→ yes | it | is / 's | in France / Brussels

→ no | where | is | it | ?
no | what | is | it | ?

44

Examples

Comparing languages

日本語

English

Real conversations

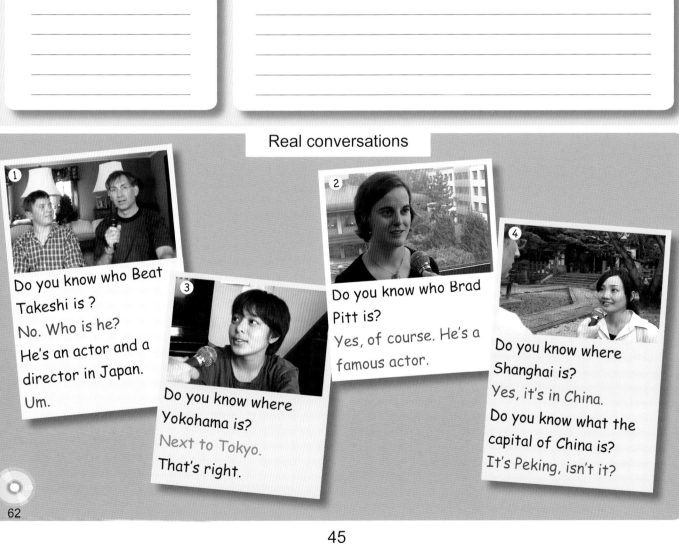

1. Do you know who Beat Takeshi is?
No. Who is he?
He's an actor and a director in Japan.
Um.

3. Do you know where Yokohama is?
Next to Tokyo.
That's right.

2. Do you know who Brad Pitt is?
Yes, of course. He's a famous actor.

4. Do you know where Shanghai is?
Yes, it's in China.
Do you know what the capital of China is?
It's Peking, isn't it?

Do you like the Giants?

ジャイアンツは好きですか？

Grammar toolbox 1

63-64

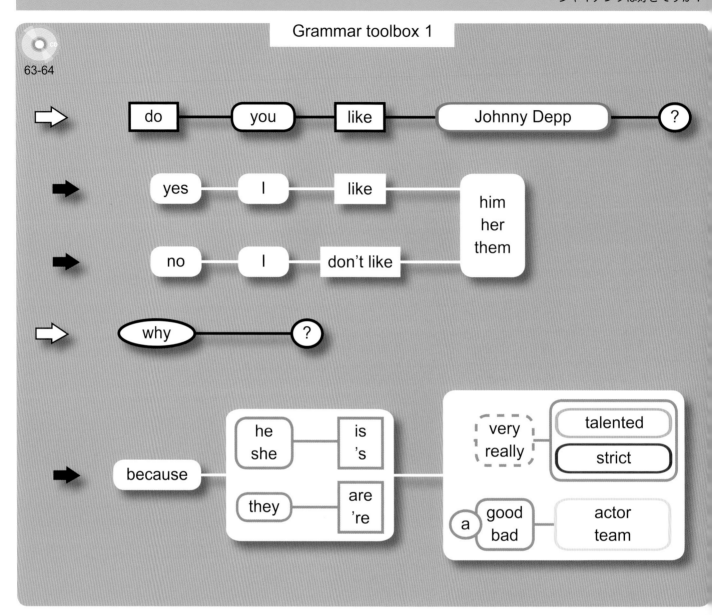

Vocabulary

Johnny Depp	ジョニーデップ	actor	俳優	talented	才能がある	strict	厳しい
Mrs.Brown		team		cool		bad	
the Giants		teacher		good		scary	

Examples

Comparing languages

日本語	English

Real conversations

Do you like Johny Depp ?
Yes, I like him.
Why?
Because he's a good actor.

Do you like Brad Pitt?
Yes, he is very good.
How about you?
Yes, he is handsome!

Do you know who Julia
Roberts is?
Yes!
Do you like her?
She is OK, but I prefer
Jennifer Lopez.

Grammar toolbox

66-67

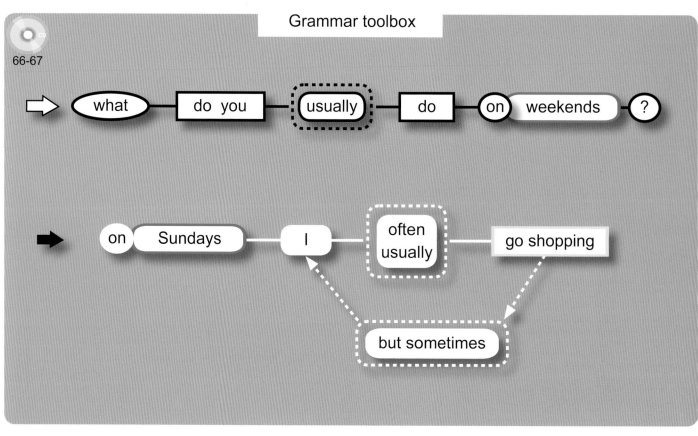

Vocabulary

Mondays	月曜日		go shopping	買い物に行く
Tuesdays			come here	
Wednesdays			have piano lessons	

Notes

Examples

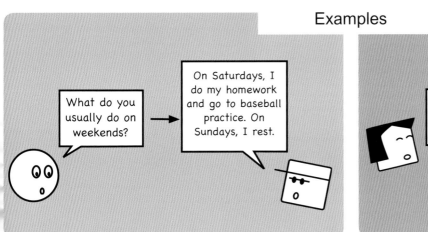

What do you usually do on weekends?

On Saturdays, I do my homework and go to baseball practice. On Sundays, I rest.

What do you usually do on Sundays?

I usually read, but sometimes I watch a video.

Comparing languages

日本語	English

Real conversations

1.
What do you usually do on week-ends?
I do my homework.

2.
What do you usually do on week-ends?
On Saturdays, I work, but on Sundays I usually go for a walk with my family.
Sounds nice.

3.
What do you usually do on the week-ends?
I go out with friends, I go shopping, and I sleep a lot.

4.
What do you usually do on Sundays?
We usually stay at home, but sometimes we go out.

68

Grammar toolbox

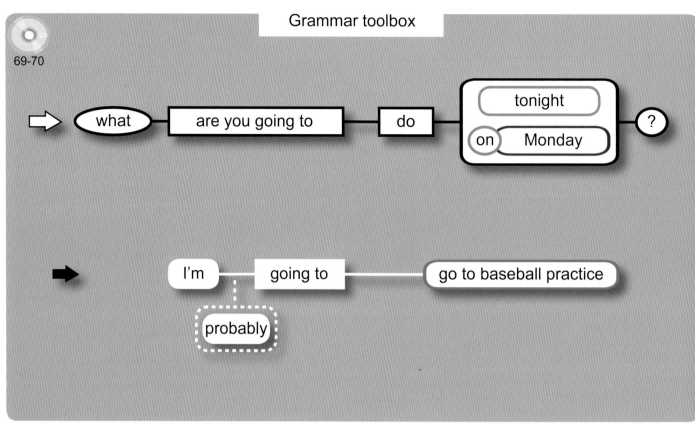

Vocabulary

Monday	月曜日
Tuesday	
Wednesday	

go to baseball practice	野球の練習に行く
read	
watch TV	

Notes

Examples

What are you going to do tonight?

I'm going to do my homework.

Good.

What are you going to do this weekend?

I'm probably going to go fishing. How about you?

I don't know yet.

Comparing languages

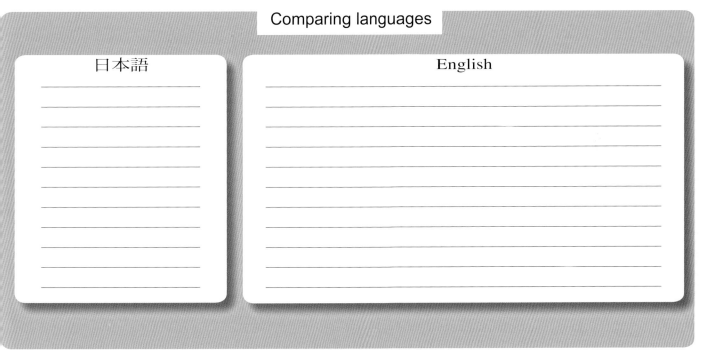

日本語

English

Real conversations

What are you going to do after school today?
I'm going to go back home and do my homework.

What are you going to do on Sunday?
Well... I'm going to go hiking.

What are you going to do this week-end?
I'm working!

What are you going to do this week-end ?
I don't know. Maybe I'll go shopping.

What did you have for breakfast?

朝食は何を食べましたか？

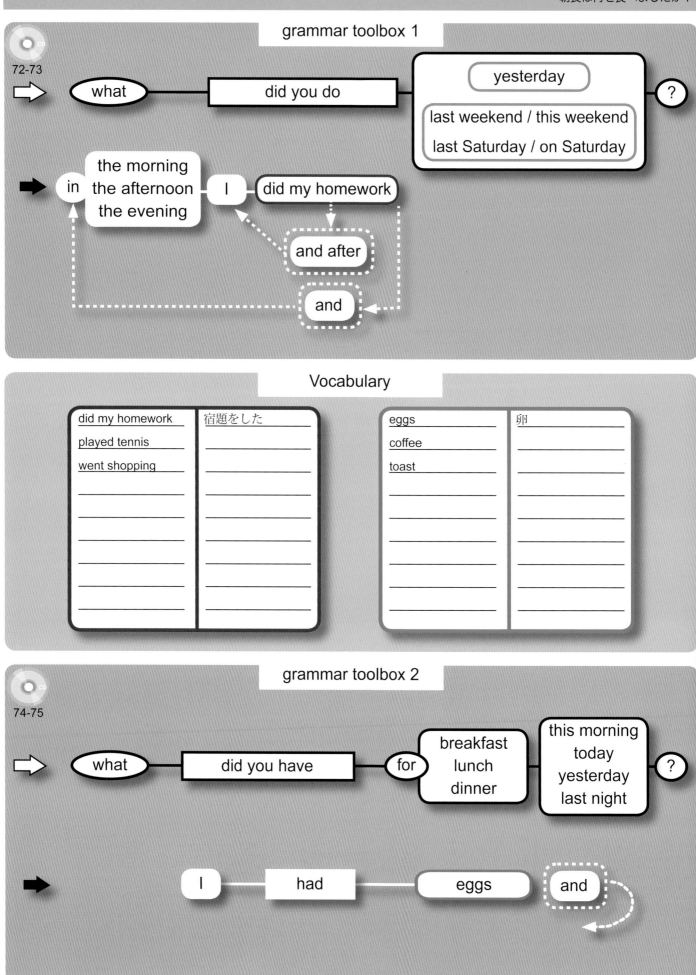

grammar toolbox 1

72-73

what — did you do — yesterday / last weekend / this weekend / last Saturday / on Saturday — ?

in the morning / the afternoon / the evening — I — did my homework — and after — and

Vocabulary

did my homework	宿題をした
played tennis	
went shopping	

eggs	卵
coffee	
toast	

grammar toolbox 2

74-75

what — did you have — for — breakfast / lunch / dinner — this morning / today / yesterday / last night — ?

I — had — eggs — and

Examples

What did you do on Sunday?

I went camping with my family.

Great!

What did you do last night?

I did my homework and went to bed.

I watched TV.

What did you have for breakfast this morning?

Eggs and toast. How about you?

I had cereal with milk.

What did you have for lunch today?

I ate rice and fish.

And what did you drink?

Japanese tea.

Comparing languages

日本語

English

Real conversations

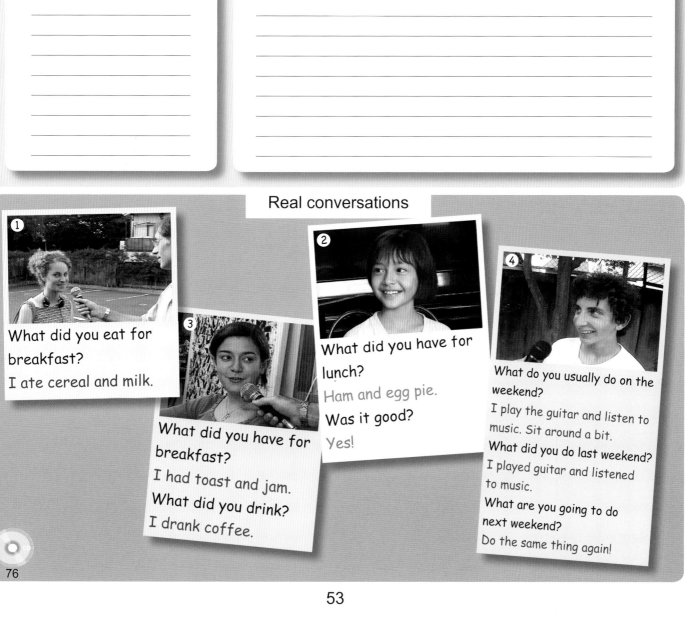

① What did you eat for breakfast?
I ate cereal and milk.

③ What did you have for breakfast?
I had toast and jam.
What did you drink?
I drank coffee.

② What did you have for lunch?
Ham and egg pie.
Was it good?
Yes!

④ What do you usually do on the weekend?
I play the guitar and listen to music. Sit around a bit.
What did you do last weekend?
I played guitar and listened to music.
What are you going to do next weekend?
Do the same thing again!

76

Write in your own conversations!

Write in your own conversations!

イミーディアット・メソッドとは？

初級会話教育のためのシンプルでダイナミックな方法で、現場の様々な困難に対応するために、日本で考案されました。様々な困難とは、例えば以下のようなものです。

● 大人数
● 学習者の消極的な態度
● 「文法はある程度勉強したけれど話せない」という学習者の特徴

もちろん、少人数クラスや話すことに積極的な学習者のクラスにも有効です。

目的は、学習者が会話の主体として実際に話せるようにすることです。

これは、1990年代に大阪大学で、複数のフランス語教師が協力し合って考案したものです。現在、日本各地の大学や高校、語学学校のフランス語教育現場に普及しています。また、ドイツ語教育、日本語教育にも適用されています。(これらの詳細はwww.almalang.com をご覧ください。)

この教科書は、イミーディアット・メソッドによる初めての英語教科書です。初級の文法事項と単語を使って、学習者が自分自身として話せるようになるためのものです。

イミーディアット・メソッドに関する詳細は、ホームページをご覧ください。

What is the Immediate Method ?

It is a simple and powerful conversation teaching method that was created in Japan in response to a challenging situation:

● large classes
● beginner or false beginner level
● cultural classroom behavior style of Japanese learners

Its objective is to have the students learn to speak in a two-way, real-time communication: in short, to take part in conversations. It was developed in Japan in the 1990's by a team of French teachers at Osaka University, and has been successfully used across Japan in universities, high schools and language schools for the teaching of French, German and Japanese as a foreign language (for those languages, see www.almalang.com). It is now being introduced to a teaching context that bears many similarities: English conversation classes for beginners and false beginners.

For a full presentation of the Immediate Method, please see our website.

http://immediate-method.com/

教科書のご注文、教師用セット(教師用指導書、ビデオ、聴解練習つきCD)のご注文の仕方は、下記のホームページをご覧ください。

To get your school to order the textbook or a teacher's set (teacher's manual, video and audio CD including listening exercises / test material), please refer them to our website:

http://www.almalang.com

Immediate conversations 1
イミーディアット・カンバセーションズ(CD付き)

2004年11月20日　初版第1版発行
2017年　3月15日　第3版第8刷発行

著者	Scott BROWN, John BREWER Nigel RANDELL, Meiko IKEZAWA Bruno VANNIEUWENHUYSE, Jean-Luc AZRA
表紙デザイン	Eric VANNIEUWENHUYSE
レイアウト	Nigel RANDELL, JuiChen TAN
発行所	ALMA Publishing 株式会社アルマ出版 www.almalang.com
ご注文・お問い合わせ	Tel: 075-203-4606 Fax: 075-320-1721 Email: info@almalang.com

© 2004 Alma Publishing　　　　Printed in Taiwan　　　　定価(本体 2095 円＋税)
ISBN 978-4-9901072-6-0